CROWN CLASSICS

LEWIS CARROLL
SELECTED POEMS

Lewis Carroll

Selected Poems

Selected and introduced by
Louise Guinness

Illustrated by John Tenniel

MOUNT ORLEANS
PRESS

Crown Classics Poetry Series
Series editor: Louise Guinness

This collection first published in 2019 by
Mount Orleans Press
23 High Street, Cricklade SN6 6AP
https://anthonyeyre.com

CIP data for this title are available from the British Library

Typography and book production by Anthony Eyre

ISBN 978-1-912945-06-1

Printed in Italy
by Esperia, Lavis (TN)

Frontispiece:

Lewis Carroll, self-portrait, 1875.
*Gernsheim Collection, Harry Ransom Center,
University of Texas at Austin*

CONTENTS

INTRODUCTION

L EWIS CARROLL was the carefully preserved pen
name of Charles Lutwidge Dodgson. Born in Cheshire
in January 1832 Dodgson was the son of a parson and
one of eleven children. He excelled at mathematics and after
a few unhappy years at Rugby school he went up to Christ
Church, Oxford in 1851. On graduating in 1855 he became
a lecturer in mathematics and stayed there for the remaining
forty-three years of his life.

The bare facts of Dodgson's uneventful life fail to illu-
minate the extraordinary work. 'Seldom are the springs
of genius so completely hidden as they are in the case of
Carroll', wrote the scholar J E Morpurgo, 'a dull family, an
uninspired schooling…the life of a celibate and almost of
a recluse, do not postulate the lavish imagination and the
wonderful humour of the Alice books and "The Hunting
of the Snark".' Carroll was certainly shy and he never
overcame a boyhood stammer. He felt more at ease in the
company of children and it was on a boating trip on a sunny
day in July 1862 with the small daughters of the Dean of
Christ Church – Lorina, Alice and Edith Liddell – that he
first began to relate the adventures of a little girl who fell
down a rabbit hole. The ten-year-old Alice then urged him to
write down the story and *Alice's Adventures in Wonderland*
was published in 1865. *Through the Looking Glass and
What Alice Found There* followed in 1872. The mock-hero-
ic poem 'The Hunting of the Snark' was published in 1876.

Carroll's later works, *Sylvie and Bruno* (1889) and *Sylvie and Bruno Concluded* (1893) failed to match the brilliance of the earlier masterpieces.

There had never been anything like the Alice books before: wonderfully free from the kind of earnest moralising that was typical of Victorian books for children at the time, the stories' narratives defy every kind convention. Most daringly of all Lewis Carroll even resisted the most basic of all restraints on a writer – that of the obligation to make sense. In the topsy-turvy worlds she travels through Alice is valiant in the cause of reason taking on one preposterous character after another, among them a white rabbit, a caterpillar, a mad-hatter, the Gryphon, a hideously ugly duchess and a Red Queen. Each one seems to conspire to bewilder her with ideas from the edge of lunacy. All the while in the roving dream stories Carroll's genius was to convey emotions deeper than laughter. Although the books were written for children adults also immediately responded to the darker notes of pathos, yearning and melancholy.

The poems are among the many surprises in the Alice books and as anything can and does happen it hardly matters when one character or another breaks into verse, moreover that those verses bear no relation whatsoever to events past or to come within the books. Alice has no idea why she has entertained the Caterpillar with eight verses of 'You are Old Father William' when she intended to recite 'How Doth the Little Busy Bee'. Nor is there any explanation for Tweedledee's disturbing tale of 'The Walrus and the Carpenter' and no warning of the shocking ending.

Carroll rose to true greatness when he unleashed himself from the constraints of language itself and in 'Jabberwocky' he created the finest nonsense verse of all time. The poem tells the story of the Jabberwock in many words newly minted from the poet's imagination and yet the poem can be read and understood by quite small children who will readily grasp the menacing quality of the Jabberwock with eyes of flame whiffling through the tulgey wood. 'Galumphing' and 'chortled' are among the words Carroll invented and 'Jabberwocky' has been translated into 65 different languages.

'The Hunting of the Snark in Eight Fits' is included here in its entirety. Carroll thought of it as a nonsense ballad for children but this is somewhat far-fatched: 'It is not children who ought to read the words of Lewis Carroll' G. K. Chesterton once wrote, '…but sages and grey-haired philosophers…in order to study that darkest problem of metaphysics, the borderland between reason and unreason, and the nature of the most erratic of spiritual forces, humour, which eternally dances between the two.' Although Carroll resisted all calls to throw light on hidden meanings within the verses generations of readers and scholars have not held back and the Snark has been the subject of reams of profound analysis and interpretations. It has also inspired many theatrical, operatic and musical adaptations and some people form Snark clubs.

The donnish Dodgson sheltered his *alter ego* from the glare of publicity and never gave interviews. 'I specially wish my face to remain unknown to the public.' He wrote to his friend A. B. Frost in 1878, 'I like my books to be known, of course: but personally I hope to remain in obscurity.'

He did, however allow Lewis Carroll an extensive correspondence with his many fans, especially children and these thousands of letters reveal his charm and playfulness. 'Don't forget the kiss to yourself, please;' he wrote to a young friend Sydney Bowlis in 1891, 'on the forehead is the best place.'

Charles Lutwidge Dodgson died of pneumonia on the 14th January in 1898, just short of his 66th birthday, but immortality has been granted to Lewis Carroll.

THE sun was shining on the sea,
    Shining with all his might:
He did his very best to make
    The billows smooth and bright—
And this was odd, because it was
    The middle of the night.

The moon was shining sulkily,
    Because she thought the sun
Had got no business to be there
    After the day was done—
'It's very rude of him', she said.
    'To come and spoil the fun!'

The sea was wet as wet could be,
    The sands were dry as dry.
You could not see a cloud, because
    No cloud was in the sky:
No birds were flying overhead—
    There were no birds to fly.

The Walrus and the Carpenter
    Were walking close at hand;
They wept like anything to see
    Such quantities of sand:
'If this were only cleared away,'
    They said, 'it *would* be grand!'

'If seven maids with seven mops
    Swept it for half a year,
Do you suppose', the Walrus said,
    'That they could get it clear?'
'I doubt it', said the Carpenter,
    And shed a bitter tear.

'O Oysters, come and walk with us!'
   The Walrus did beseech.
'A pleasant walk, a pleasant talk,
   Along the briny beach:
We cannot do with more than four,
   To give a hand to each.'

The eldest Oyster looked at him,
   But never a word he said:
The eldest Oyster winked his eye,
   And shook his heavy head—
Meaning to say he did not choose
   To leave the oyster-bed.

But four young Oysters hurried up,
   All eager for the treat:
Their coats were brushed, their faces washed,
   Their shoes were clean and neat—
And this was odd, because, you know,
   They hadn't any feet.

Four other Oysters followed them,
    And yet another four;
And thick and fast they came at last,
    And more, and more, and more—
All hopping through the frothy waves,
    And scrambling to the shore.

The Walrus and the Carpenter
    Walked on a mile or so,
And then they rested on a rock
    Conveniently low:
And all the little Oysters stood
    And waited in a row.

'The time has come', the Walrus said,
    'To talk of many things:
Of shoes—and ships—and sealing-wax—
    Of cabbages—and kings—
And why the sea is boiling hot—
And whether pigs have wings.'

'But, wait a bit,' the Oysters cried,
    'Before we have our chat;
For some of us are out of breath,
    And all of us are fat!'
'No hurry!' said the Carpenter.
    They thanked him much for that.

'A loaf of bread', the Walrus said,
    'Is what we chiefly need:
Pepper and vinegar besides
    Are very good indeed—
Now if you're ready. Oysters dear,
    We can begin to feed.'

'But not on us!' the Oysters cried,
　　Turning a little blue,
'After such kindness, that would be
　　A dismal thing to do!'
'The night is fine', the Walrus said.
　　'Do you admire the view?

'It was so kind of you to come!
　　And you are very nice!'
The Carpenter said nothing but
　　'Cut us another slice:
I wish you were not quite so deaf—
　　I've had to ask you twice!'

'It seems a shame', the Walrus said,
　　'To play them such a trick.
After we've brought them out so far,
　　And made them trot so quick!'
The Carpenter said nothing but
　　'The butter's spread too thick!'

'I weep for you', the Walrus said:
　　'I deeply sympathise.'
With sobs and tears he sorted out
　　Those of the largest size,
Holding his pocket-handkerchief
　　Before his streaming eyes.

'O Oysters,' said the Carpenter,
　　'You've had a pleasant run!
Shall we be trotting home again?'
　　But answer came there none—
And this was scarcely odd, because
　　They'd eaten every one.

IMPORTANT EVIDENCE

THEY told me you had been to her,
And mentioned me to him:
She gave me a good character,
But said I could not swim.

He sent them word I had not gone,
(We know it to be true):
If she should push the matter on,
What would become of you?

I gave her one, they gave him two,
You gave us three or more;
They all returned from him to you,
Though they were mine before.

If I or she should chance to be
Involved in this affair,
He trusts to you to set them free,
Exactly as we were.

My notion was that you had been
(Before she had this fit)
An obstacle that came between
Him, and ourselves, and it.

Don't let him know she liked them best,
For this must ever be
A secret, kept from all the rest,
Between yourself and me.

THE OLD SONG

TWEEDLEDUM and Tweedledee
   Agreed to have a battle;
For Tweedledum said Tweedledee
   Had spoiled his nice new rattle.

Just then flew down a monstrous crow,
   As black as a tar-barrel;
Which frightened both the heroes so,
   They quite forgot their quarrel.

A SEA DIRGE

THERE are certain things—as, a spider, a ghost,
　　The income-tax, gout, an umbrella for three—
That I hate, but the thing that I hate the most
　　Is a thing they call the Sea.

Pour some salt water over the floor—
　　Ugly I'm sure you'll allow it to be:
Suppose it extended a mile or more
　　That's very like the Sea.

Beat a dog till it howls outright—
　　Cruel, but all very well for a spree:
Suppose that he did so day and night,
　　That would be like the Sea.

I had a vision of nursery-maids;
　　Tens of thousands passed by me—
All leading children with wooden spades,
　　And this was by the Sea.

Who invented those spades of wood?
　　Who was it cut them out of the tree?
None, I think, but an idiot could—
　　Or one that loved the Sea.

It is pleasant and dreamy, no doubt, to float
　　With 'thoughts as boundless, and souls as free':
But, suppose you are very unwell in the boat,
　　How do you like the Sea?

There is an insect that people avoid
　　(Whence is derived the verb 'to flee').
Where have you been by it most annoyed?
　　In lodgings by the Sea.

If you like your coffee with sand for dregs,
  A decided hint of salt in your tea,
And a fishy taste in the very eggs—
  By all means choose the Sea.

And if, with these dainties to drink and eat,
  You prefer not a vestige of grass or tree,
And a chronic state of wet in your feet,
  Then—I recommend the Sea.

For *I* have friends who dwell by the coast—
  Pleasant friends they are to me!
It is when I am with them I wonder most
  That anyone likes the Sea.

A-SITTING ON A GATE

I'LL tell thee everything I can;
  There's little to relate.
I saw an aged aged man,
  A-sitting on a gate.
'Who are you, aged man?' I said.
  'And how is it you live?'
And his answer trickled through my head
  Like water through a sieve.

He said, 'I look for butterflies
  That sleep among the wheat:
I make them into mutton pies,
  And sell them in the street.
I sell them unto men', he said,
  'Who sail on stormy seas;
And that's the way I get my bread—
  A trifle, if you please.'

But I was thinking of a plan
   To dye one's whiskers green,
And always use so large a fan
   That they could not be seen.
So, having no reply to give
   To what the old man said,
I cried, 'Come, tell me how you live!'
   And thumped him on the head.

His accents mild took up the tale:
   He said, 'I go my ways,
And when I find a mountain-rill,
   I set it in a blaze;
And thence they make a stuff they call
Rowlands' Macassar Oil—
   Yet twopence-halfpenny is all
They give me for my toil.'

But I was thinking of a way
    To feed oneself on batter,
And so go on from day to day
    Getting a little fatter.
I shook him well from side to side,
    Until his face was blue:
'Come, tell me how you live,' I cried,
    'And what it is you do!'

He said, 'I hunt for haddocks' eyes
    Among the heather bright,
And work them into waistcoat-buttons
    In the silent night.
And these I do not sell for gold
    Or coin of silvery shine,
But for a copper halfpenny,
    And that will purchase nine.

'I sometimes dig for buttered rolls,
    Or set limed twigs for crabs:
I sometimes search for grassy knolls
    For wheels of Hansom-cabs.
And that's the way' (he gave a wink)
    'By which I get my wealth—
And very gladly will I drink
    Your Honour's noble health.'

I heard him then, for I had just
    Completed my design
To keep the Menai bridge from rust
    By boiling it in wine.
I thanked him much for telling me
    The way he got his wealth,
But chiefly for his wish that he
    Might drink my noble health.

And now, if e'er by chance I put
   My fingers into glue,
Or madly squeeze a right-hand foot
   Into a left-hand shoe,
Or if I drop upon my toe
   A very heavy weight,
I weep, for it reminds me so
Of that old man I used to know—
Whose look was mild, whose speech was slow,
Whose hair was whiter than the snow,
Whose face was very like a crow,
With eye, like cinders, all aglow,
Who seemed distracted with his woe,
Who rocked his body to and fro,
And muttered mumblingly and low,
As if his mouth were full of dough,
Who snorted like a buffalo—
That summer evening long ago
   A-sitting on a gate.

JABBERWOCKY

T'was brillig, and the slithy toves
    Did gyre and gimble in the wabe;
All mimsy were the borogoves,
    And the mome raths outgrabe.

'Beware the Jabberwock, my son!
    The jaws that bite, the claws that catch!
Beware the Jubjub bird, and shun
    The frumious Bandersnatch!'

He took his vorpal sword in hand:
    Long time the manxome foe he sought—
So rested he by the Tumtum tree,
And stood awhile in thought.

And as in uffish thought he stood,
    The Jabberwock, with eyes of flame,
Came whiflling through the tulgey wood,
    And burbled as it came!

One, two! One, two! And through and through
    The vorpal blade went snicker-snack!
He left it dead, and with its head
    He went galumphing back.

'And hast thou slain the Jabberwock?
    Come to my arms, my beamish boy!
O frabjous day! Callooh! Callay!'
    He chortled in his joy.

'Twas brillig, and the slithy toves
    Did gyre and gimble in the wabe;
All mimsy were the borogoves.
    And the mome raths outgrabe.

THE HUNTING OF THE SNARK

An Agony in Eight Fits

FIT THE FIRST

THE LANDING

'JUST the place for a Snark!' the Bellman cried,
    As he landed his crew with care;
Supporting each man on the top of the tide
    By a finger entwined in his hair.

'Just the place for a Snark! I have said it twice:
    That alone should encourage the crew.
Just the place for a Snark!—I have said it thrice:
    What I tell you three times is true.'

The crew was complete: it included a Boots—
    A maker of Bonnets and Hoods—
A Barrister, brought to arrange their disputes—
    And a Broker, to value their goods.

A Billiard-marker, whose skill was immense,
    Might perhaps have won more than his share—
But a Banker, engaged at enormous expense,
    Had the whole of their cash in his care.

There was also a Beaver, that paced on the deck,
    Or would sit making lace in the bow:
And had often (the Bellman said) saved them from wreck,
    Though none of the sailors knew how.

There was one who was famed for the number of things
    He forgot when he entered the ship:
His umbrella, his watch, all his jewels and rings,
    And the clothes he had bought for the trip.

He had forty-two boxes, all carefully packed,
    With his name painted clearly on each :
But, since he omitted to mention the fact,
    They were all left behind on the beach.

The loss of his clothes hardly mattered, because
    He had seven coats on when he came,
With three pair of boots—but the worst of it was,
    He had wholly forgotten his name.

He would answer to 'Hi!' or to any loud cry,
    Such as 'Fry me!' or 'Fritter my wig!'
To 'What-you-may-call-um!' or 'What-was-his-name!'
    But especially' 'Thing-um-a-jig!'

While, for those who preferred a more forcible word,
    He had different names from these:
His intimate friends called him 'Candle-ends'.
    And his enemies 'Toasted-cheese'.

'His form is ungainly—his intellect small—'
    (So the Bellman would often remark)
'But his courage is perfect! And that, after all,
    Is the thing that one needs with a Snark.'

He would joke with hyrenas, returning their stare
    With an impudent wag of the head:
And he once went a walk, paw-in-paw, with a bear,
    'Just to keep up its spirits', he said.

He came as a Baker : but owned when too late—
    And it drove the poor Bellman half-mad—
He could only bake Bridecake—for which, I may state,
    No materials were to be had.

The last of the crew needs especial remark,
    Though he looked an incredible dunce:
He had just one idea—but, that one being 'Snark',
    The good Bellman engaged him at once.

He came as a Butcher: but gravely declared,
    When the ship had been sailing a week,
He could only kill Beavers. The Bellman looked scared,
    And was almost too frightened to speak:

But at length he explained, in a tremulous tone,
    There was only one Beaver on board;
And that was a tame one he had of his own,
    Whose death would be deeply deplored.

The Beaver, who happened to hear the remark,
    Protested, with tears in its eyes,
That not even the rapture of hunting the Snark
    Could atone for that dismal surprise !

It strongly advised that the Butcher should be
    Conveyed in a separate ship:
But the Bellman declared that would never agree
    With the plans he had made for the trip:

Navigation was always a difficult art,
    Though with only one ship and one bell:
And he feared he must really decline, for his part,
    Undertaking another as well.

The Beaver's best course was, no doubt, to procure
    A second-hand dagger-proof coat—
So the Baker advised it—and next, to insure
    Its life in some Office of note:

This the Banker suggested, and offered for hire
    (On moderate terms), or for sale,
Two excellent Policies, one Against Fire,
    And one Against Damage From Hail.

Yet still, ever after that sorrowful day,
    Whenever the Butcher was by,
The Beaver kept looking the opposite way,
    And appeared unaccountably shy.

FIT THE SECOND

THE BELLMAN'S SPEECH

THE Bellman himself they all praised to the skies—
  Such a carriage, such ease and such grace!
Such solemnity, too! One could see he was wise,
  The moment one looked in his face!

He had bought a large map representing the sea,
  Without the least vestige of land:
And the crew were much pleased when they found it to be
  A map they could all understand.

'What's the good of Mercator's North Poles and Equators,
  Tropics, Zones, and Meridian Lines?'
So the Bellman would cry: and the crew would reply
  'They are merely conventional signs!

'Other maps are such shapes, with their islands and capes!
  But we've got our brave Captain to thank'
(So the crew would protest) 'that he's bought us the best—
  A perfect and absolute blank! '

This was charming, no doubt; but they shortly found out
  That the Captain they trusted so well
Had only one notion for crossing the ocean,
  And that was to tingle his bell.

He was thoughtful and grave—but the orders he gave
  Were enough to bewilder a crew.
When he cried, 'Steer to starboard, but keep her head larboard!'
  What on earth was the helmsman to do?

Then the bowsprit got mixed with the rudder sometimes:
  A thing, as the Bellman remarked,
That frequently happens in tropical climes,
  When a vessel is, so to speak, 'snarked'.

27

But the principal failing occurred in the sailing,
    And the Bellman, perplexed and distressed,
Said he *had* hoped, at least, when the wind blew due East
    That the ship would *not* travel due West!

But the danger was past-they had landed at last,
    With their boxes, portmanteaus, and bags:
Yet at first sight the crew were not pleased with the view,
    Which consisted of chasms and crags.

The Bellman perceived that their spirits were low,
    And repeated in musical tone
Some jokes he had kept for a season of woe—
    But the crew would do nothing but groan.

He served out some grog with a liberal hand,
    And bade them sit down on the beach:
And they could not but own that their Captain looked grand,
    As he stood and delivered his speech.

'Friends, Romans, and countrymen, lend me your ears!'
    (They were all of them fond of quotations:
So they drank to his health, and they gave him three cheers,
    While he served out additional rations).

'We have sailed many months, we have sailed many weeks,
    (Four weeks to the month you may mark),
But never as yet ('tis your Captain who speaks)
    Have we caught the least glimpse of a Snark!

'We have sailed many weeks, we have sailed many days
    (Seven days to the week I allow),
But a Snark, on the which we might lovingly gaze,
    We have never beheld till now!

'Come, listen, my men, while I tell you again
   The five unmistakable marks
By which you may know, wheresoever you go,
   The warranted genuine Snarks.

'Let us take them in order. The first is the taste,
   Which is meagre and hollow, but crisp:
Like a coat that is rather too tight in the waist,
   With a flavour of Will-o'-the-wisp.

'It's habit of getting up late you'll agree
   That it carries too far, when I say
That it frequently breakfasts at five-o'clock tea,
   And dines on the following day.

'The third is its slowness in taking a jest,
   Should you happen to venture on one,
It will sigh like a thing that is deeply distressed:
   And it always looks grave at a pun.

'The fourth is its fondness for bathing-machines,
   Which it constantly carries about,
And believes that they add to the beauty of scenes—
   A sentiment open to doubt.

'The fifth is ambition. It next will be right
   To describe each particular batch:
Distinguishing those that have feathers, and bite,
   From those that have whiskers, and scratch.

'For, although common Snarks do no manner of harm,
   Yet I feel it my duty to say,
Some are Boojums—' The Bellman broke off in alarm,
   For the Baker had fainted away.

FIT THE THIRD

THE BAKER'S TALE

THEY roused him with muffins—they roused him with ice—
    They roused him with mustard and cress—
They roused him with jam and judicious advice—
    They set him conundrums to guess.

When at length he sat up and was able to speak,
    His sad story he offered to tell;
And the Bellman cried, 'Silence! not even a shriek!'
    And excitedly tingled his bell.

There was silence supreme! Not a shriek, not a scream,
    Scarcely even a howl or a groan,
As the man they called 'Ho!' told his story of woe
    In an antediluvian tone.

'My father and mother were honest, though poor—'
    'Skip all that!' cried the Bellman in haste.
'If it once becomes dark, there's no chance of a Snark—
    We have hardly a minute to waste!'

'I skip forty years.' said the Baker, in tears,
    'And proceed without further remark
To the day when you took me aboard of your ship
    To help you in hunting the Snark.

'A dear uncle of mine (after whom I was named)
    Remarked, when I bade him farewell—'
'Oh, skip your dear uncle!' the Bellman exclaimed,
    As he angrily tingled his bell.

'He remarked to me then,' said that mildest of men,
    '"If your Snark be a Snark, that is right:
Fetch it home by all means—you may serve it with greens,
    And it's handy for striking a light.

'"You may seek it with thimbles—and seek it with care;
    You may hunt it with forks and hope;
You may threaten its life with a railway-share;
    You may charm it with smiles and soap-"'

('That's exactly the method,' the Bellman bold
    In a hasty parenthesis cried,
'That's exactly the way I have always been told
    That the capture of Snarks should be tried!')

'"But oh, beamish nephew, beware of the day,
    If your Snark be a Boojum; for then
You will softly and suddenly vanish away,
    And never be met with again!"

'It is this, it is this that oppresses my soul,
    When I think of my uncle's last words:
And my heart is like nothing so much as a bowl
    Brimming over with quivering curds!'

'"It is this, it is this—" We have had that before!'
    The Bellman indignantly said.
And the Baker replied, 'Let me say it once more.
    It is this, it is this that I dread!

'I engage with the Snark—every night after dark—
    In a dreamy delirious fight:
I serve it with greens in those shadowy scenes,
    And I use it for striking a light;

'But if ever I meet with a Boojum, that day,
    In a moment (of this I am sure),
I shall softly and suddenly vanish away—
    And the notion I cannot endure!'

LEWIS CARROLL

FIT THE FOURTH

THE HUNTING

THE Bellman looked uffish, and wrinkled his brow.
    'If only you'd spoken before!
It's excessively awkward to mention it now.
    With the Snark, so to speak, at the door!

'We should all of us grieve, as you well may believe.
    If you never were met with again—
But surely, my man, when the voyage began,
    You might have suggested it then?

'It's excessively awkward to mention it now
    As I think I've already remarked.'
And the man they called 'Hi!' replied, with a sigh,
    'I informed you the day we embarked.

'You may charge me with murder—or want of sense—
    (We are all of us weak at times):
But the slightest approach to a false pretence
    Was never among my crimes!

'I said it in Hebrew—I said it in Dutch—
    I said it in German and Greek;
But I wholly forgot (and it vexes me much)
    That English is what you speak!'

''Tis a pitiful tale,' said the Bellman, whose face
    Had grown longer at every word;
'But, now that you've stated the whole of your case,
    More debate would be simply absurd.

'The rest of my speech' (he explained to his men)
    'You shall hear when I've leisure to speak it.
But the Snark is at hand, let me tell you again!
    'Tis your glorious duty to seek it!

32

'To seek it with thimbles, to seek it with care;
　　To pursue it with forks and hope;
To threaten its life with a railway-share;
　　To charm it with smiles and soap!

'For the Snark's a peculiar creature, that won't
　　Be caught in a commonplace way.
Do all that you know, and try all that you don't:
　　Not a chance must be wasted to-day!

'For England expects—I forbear to proceed:
　　'Tis a maxim tremendous, but trite:
And you'd best be unpacking the things that you need
　　To rig yourselves out for a fight.'

Then the Banker endorsed a blank cheque (which he crossed),
　　And changed his loose silver for notes.
The Baker with care combed his whiskers and hair,
　　And shook the dust out of his coats.

The Boots and the Broker were sharpening a spade—
　　Each working the grindstone in turn;
But the Beaver went on making lace, and displayed
　　No interest in the concern.

Though the Barrister tried to appeal to its pride,
　　And vainly proceeded to cite
A number of cases, in which making laces
　　Had been proved an infringement of right.

The maker of Bonnets ferociously planned
　　A novel arrangement of bows :
While the Billiard-marker with quivering hand
　　Was chalking the tip of his nose.

But the Butcher turned nervous, and dressed himself fine,
　　With yellow kid gloves and a ruff—
Said he felt it exactly like going to dine,
　　Which the Bellman declared was all 'stuff'.

33

'Introduce me, now there's a good fellow,' he said,
    'If we happen to meet it together!'
And the Bellman, sagaciously nodding his head,
    Said, 'That must depend on the weather'.

The Beaver went simply galumphing about,
    At seeing the Butcher so shy:
And even the Baker, though stupid and stout,
    Made an effort to wink with one eye.

'Be a man!' said the Bellman in wrath, as he heard
    The Butcher beginning to sob.
'Should we meet with a Jubjub, that desperate bird,
    We shall need all our strength for the job!'

FIT THE FIFTH

THE BEAVER'S LESSON

THEY sought it with thimbles, they sought it with care;
    They pursued it with forks and hope;
They threatened its life with a railway-share;
    They charmed it with smiles and soap.

Then the Butcher contrived an ingenious plan
    For making a separate sally;
And had fixed on a spot unfrequented by man,
    A dismal and desolate valley.

But the very same plan to the Beaver occurred:
    It had chosen the very same place;
Yet neither betrayed, by a sign or a word,
    The disgust that appeared in his face.

Each thought he was thinking of nothing but 'Snark'
   And the glorious work of the day;
And each tried to pretend that he did not remark
   That the other was going that way.

But the valley grew narrower and narrower still,
   And the evening got darker and colder,
Till (merely from nervousness, not from goodwill)
   They marched along shoulder to shoulder.

Then a scream, shrill and high, rent the shuddering sky,
   And they knew that some danger was near:
The Beaver turned pale to the tip of his tail,
   And even the Butcher felt queer.

He thought of his childhood, left far far behind—
   That blissful and innocent state—
The sound so exactly recalled to his mind
   A pencil that squeaks on a slate!

''Tis the voice of the Jubjub!' he suddenly cried
   (This man, that they used to call 'Dunce').
'As the Bellman would tell you,' he added with pride,
   'I have uttered that sentiment once.

''Tis the note of the Jubjub! Keep count, I entreat;
   You will find I have told it you twice.
'Tis the song of the Jubjub! The proof is complete
   If only I've stated it thrice.'

The Beaver had counted with scrupulous care,
   Attending to every word:
But it fairly lost heart, and outgrabe in despair,
   When the third repetition occurred.

It felt that, in spite of all possible pains,
   It had somehow contrived to lose count,
And the only thing now was to rack its poor brains
   By reckoning up the amount.

'Two added to one—if that could but be done'.
　　It said, 'with one's fingers and thumbs!'
Recollecting with tears how, in earlier years,
　　It had taken no pains with its sums.

'The thing can be done', said the Butcher, 'I think
　　The thing must be done, I am sure.
The thing shall be done! Bring me paper and ink,
　　The best there is time to procure.'

The Beaver brought paper, portfolio, pens,
　　And ink in unfailing supplies:
While strange creepy creatures came of their dens,
　　And watched them with wondering eyes.

So engrossed was the Butcher, he heeded them not,
　　As he wrote with a pen in each hand,
And explained all the while in a popular style
　　Which the Beaver could well understand.

'Taking Three as the subject to reason about—
　　A convenient number to state—
We add Seven, and Ten, and then multiply out
　　By One Thousand diminished by Eight.

'The result we proceed to divide, as you see,
　　By Nine Hundred and Ninety and Two:
Then subtract Seventeen, and the answer must be
　　Exactly and perfectly true.

'The method employed I would gladly explain,
　　While I have it so clear in my head,
If I had but the time and you had but the brain—
　　But much yet remains to be said.

'In one moment I've seen what has hitherto been
　　Enveloped in absolute mystery,
And without extra charge I will give you at large
　　A Lesson in Natural History.'

In his genial way he proceeded to say
    (Forgetting all laws of propriety,
And that giving instruction, without introduction,
    Would have caused quite a thrill in Society),

'As to temper the Jubjub's a desperate bird,
    Since it lives in perpetual passion:
Its taste in costume is entirely absurd—
    It is ages ahead of the fashion :

'But it knows any friend it has met once before:
    It never will look at a bribe:
And in charity-meetings it stands at the door,
    And collects—though it does not subscribe.

'Its flavour when cooked is more exquisite far
    Than mutton, or oysters, or eggs:
(Some think it keeps best in an ivory jar,
    And some, in mahogany kegs):

'You boil it in sawdust: you salt it in glue:
    You condense it with locusts and tape:
Still keeping one principal object in view—
    To preserve its symmetrical shape.'

The Butcher would gladly have talked till next day,
    But he felt that the Lesson must end,
And he wept with delight in attempting to say
    He considered the Beaver his friend.

While the Beaver confessed, with affectionate looks
    More eloquent even than tears,
It had learnt in ten minutes far more than all books
    Would have taught it in seventy years.

They returned hand-in-hand, and the Bellman, unmanned
    (For a moment) with noble emotion,
Said, 'This amply repays all the wearisome days
    We have spent on the billowy ocean!'

Such friends, as the Beaver and Butcher became,
  Have seldom if ever been known;
In winter or summer, 'twas always the same—
  You could never meet either alone.

And when quarrels arose—as one frequently finds
  Quarrels will, spite of every endeavour—
The song of the Jubjub recurred to their minds,
  And cemented their friendship for ever!

FIT THE SIXTH

THE BARRISTER'S DREAM

THEY sought it with thimbles, they sought it with care;
  They pursued it with forks and hope;
They threatened its life with a railway-share;
  They charmed it with smiles and soap.

But the Barrister, weary of proving in vain
  That the Beaver's lace-making was wrong,
Fell asleep, and in dreams saw the creature quite plain
  That his fancy had dwelt on so long.

He dreamed that he stood in a shadowy Court,
  Where the Snark, with a glass in its eye,
Dressed in gown, bands, and wig, was defending a pig
  On the charge of deserting its sty.

The Witnesses proved, without error or flaw,
  That the sty was deserted when found:
And the Judge kept explaining the state of the law
  In a soft under-current of sound.

The indictment had never been clearly expressed,
  And it seemed that the Snark had begun,
And had spoken three hours, before anyone guessed
  What the pig was supposed to have done.

The Jury had each formed a different view
  (Long before the indictment was read),
And they all spoke at once, so that none of them knew
  One word that the others had said.

'You must know—' said the Judge: but the Snark
            exclaimed, 'Fudge!
  That statute is obsolete quite!
Let me tell you, my friends, the whole question depends
  On an ancient manorial right.

'In the matter of Treason the pig would appear
  To have aided, but scarcely abetted:
While the charge of Insolvency fails, it is clear,
  If you grant the plea "never indebted".

'The fact of Desertion I will not dispute:
  But its guilt, as I trust, is removed
(So far as relates to the costs of this suit)
  By the Alibi which has been proved.

'My poor client's fate now depends on your votes.'
  Here the speaker sat down in his place,
And directed the Judge to refer to his notes
  And briefly to sum up the case.

But the Judge said he never had summed up before;
  So the Snark undertook it instead,
And summed it so well that it came to far more
  Than the Witnesses ever had said!

When the verdict was called for, the Jury declined,
  As the word was so puzzling to spell;
But they ventured to hope that the Snark wouldn't mind
  Undertaking that duty as well.

So the Snark found the verdict, although as it owned,
　　It was spent with the toils of the day:
When it said the word, 'GUILTY!' the Jury all groaned,
　　And some of them fainted away.

Then the Snark pronounced sentence, the Judge being quite
　　Too nervous to utter a word:
When it rose to its feet, there was silence like night,
　　And the fall of a pin might be heard.

'Transportation for life' was the sentence it gave,
　　'And *then* to be fined forty pound.'
The Jury all cheered, though the Judge said he feared
　　That the phrase was not legally sound.

But their wild exultation was suddenly checked
　　When the jailer informed them, with tears,
Such a sentence would have not the slightest effect,
　　As the pig had been dead for some years.

The Judge left the Court, looking deeply disgusted:
　　But the Snark, though a little aghast,
As the lawyer to whom the defence was entrusted,
　　Went bellowing on to the last.

Thus the Barrister dreamed, while the bellowing seemed
　　To grow every moment more clear:
Till he woke to the knell of a furious bell,
　　Which the Bellman rang close at his ear.

FIT THE SEVENTH

THE BANKER'S FATE

THEY sought it with thimbles, they sought it with care;
  They pursued it with forks and hope;
They threatened its life with a railway-share;
  They charmed it with smiles and soap.

And the Banker, inspired with a courage so new
  It was matter for general remark,
Rushed madly ahead and was lost to their view
  In his zeal to discover the Snark.

But while he was seeking with thimbles and care,
  A Bandersnatch swiftly drew nigh
And grabbed at the Banker, who shrieked in despair,
  For he knew it was useless to fly.

He offered large discount—he offered a cheque
  (Drawn 'to bearer') for seven-pounds-ten:
But the Bandersnatch merely extended its neck
  And grabbed at the Banker again.

Without rest or pause—while those frumious jaws
  Went savagely snapping around—
He skipped and he hopped, and he floundered and flopped,
  Till fainting he fell to the ground.

The Bandersnatch fled as the others appeared:
  Led on by that fear-stricken yell:
And the Bellman remarked, 'It is just as I feared!'
  And solemnly tolled on his bell.

He was black in the face, and they scarcely could trace
  The least likeness to what he had been:
While so great was his fright that his waistcoat turned white—
  A wonderful thing to be seen!

To the horror of all who were present that day,
　He uprose in full evening dress,
And with senseless grimaces endeavoured to say
　What his tongue could no longer express.

Down he sank in a chair—ran his hands through his hair—
　And chanted in mimsiest tones
Words whose utter inanity proved his insanity,
　While he rattled a couple of bones.

'Leave him here to his fate—it is getting so late!'
　The Bellman exclaimed in a fright.
'We have lost half the day. Any further delay,
　And we shan't catch a Snark before night!'

FIT THE EIGHTH

THE VANISHING

THEY sought it with thimbles, they sought it with care;
　They pursued it with forks and hope;
They threatened its life with a railway-share;
　They charmed it with smiles and soap.

They shuddered to think that the chase might fail,
　And the Beaver, excited at last,
Went bounding along on the tip of its tail,
　For the daylight was nearly past.

'There is Thingumbob shouting!' the Bellman said.
　'He is shouting like mad, only hark!
He is waving his hands, he is wagging his head,
　He has certainly found a Snark!'

They gazed in delight, while the Butcher exclaimed,
    'He was always a desperate wag!'
They beheld him—their Baker—their hero unnamed—
    On the top of a neighbouring crag,

Erect and sublime, for one moment of time.
    In the next, that wild figure they saw
(As if stung by a spasm) plunge into a chasm,
    While they waited and listened in awe.

'It's a Snark!' was the sound that first came to their ears,
    And seemed almost too good to be true.
Then followed a torrent of laughter and cheers:
    Then the ominous words, 'It's a Boo—'

Then, silence. Some fancied they heard in the air
    A weary and wandering sigh
That sounded like '–jum!' but the others declare
    It was only a breeze that went by.

They hunted till darkness came on, but they found
    Not a button, or feather, or mark,
By which they could tell that they stood on the ground
    Where the Baker had met with the Snark.

In the midst of the word he was trying to say
    In the midst of his laughter and glee,
He had softly and suddenly vanished away —
    For the Snark *was* a Boojum, you see.

HUMPTY DUMPTY'S SONG

In winter, when the fields are white,
I sing this song for your delight—

In spring, when woods are getting green,
I'll try and tell you what I mean.

In summer, when the days are long,
Perhaps you'll understand the song:

In autumn, when the leaves are brown,
Take pen and ink and write it down.

I sent a message to the fish:
I told them, 'This is what I wish.'

The little fishes of the sea,
They sent an answer back to me.

The little fishes' answer was,
'We cannot do it, Sir, because—'

I sent to them again to say,
'It will be better to obey.'

The fishes answered with a grin,
'Why, what a temper you are in!'

I told them once, I told them twice:
They would not listen to advice.

I took a kettle large and new,
Fit for the deed I had to do.

My heart went hop, my heart went thump;
I filled the kettle at the pump.

Then someone came to me and said,
'The little fishes are in bed.'

I said to him, I said it plain,
'Then you must wake them up again.'

I said it very loud and clear;
I went and shouted in his ear.

But he was very stiff and proud;
He said, 'You needn't shout so loud!'

And he was very proud and stiff;
He said, 'I'd go and wake them, if—'

I took a corkscrew from the shelf:
I went to wake them up myself.

And when I found the door was locked,
I pulled and pushed and kicked and knocked.

And when I found the door was shut,
I tried to turn the handle, but—

FURY AND THE MOUSE

Fury said to a
mouse. That he
met in the
house. 'Let
us both go
to law: *I*
will prose-
cute *you*.
Come, I'll
take no de-
nial; We must
have a trial:
For really
this morn-
ing I've no-
thing to do.'
Said the
mouse to the
cur, 'Such a
trial, dear
Sir, With
no jury or
judge, would
be wasting
our breath.'
'I'll be judge,
I'll be jury,'
Said cun-
ning old
Fury: 'I'll
try the
whole
cause and
condemn
you to
death.'

HE THOUGHT HE SAW

HE thought he saw an Elephant,
That practised on a fife:
He looked again, and found it was
A letter from his wife.
'At length I realise', he said,
'The bitterness of Life.'

He thought he saw a Buffalo
Upon the chimney-piece:
He looked again, and found it was
His Sister's Husband's Niece.
'Unless you leave this house,' he said,
'I'll send for the Police!'

He thought he saw a Rattlesnake
That questioned him in Greek:
He looked again, and found it was
The Middle of Next Week.
'The one thing I regret', he said,
'Is that it cannot speak!'

He thought he saw a Banker's Clerk
Descending from the bus:
He looked again, and found it was
A Hippopotamus:
'If this should stay to dine,' he said,
'There won't be much for us!'

He thought he saw a Coach-and-Four
That stood beside his bed:
He looked again, and found it was
A Bear without a Head.
'Poor thing,' he said, 'poor silly thing!
It's waiting to be fed!'

He thought he saw an Albatross
That fluttered round the lamp:
He looked again, and found it was
A Penny-Postage-Stamp.
'You'd best be getting home,' he said;
'The nights are very damp!'

He thought he saw a Garden-Door
That opened with a key:
He looked again, and found it was
A double Rule of Three.
'And all its mystery', he said,
'Is clear as day to me!'

He thought he saw an Argument
That proved he was the Pope:
He looked again, and found it was
A Bar of Mottled Soap.
'A fact so dread', he faintly said,
'Extinguishes all hope!'

'TIS THE VOICE OF THE LOBSTER

'Tis the voice of the Lobster; I heard him declare.
'You have baked me too brown, I must sugar my hair.'
As a duck with its eyelids, so he with his nose
Trims his belt and his buttons, and turns out his toes.
When the sands are all dry, he is gay as a lark,
And will talk in contemptuous tones of the Shark :
But. when the tide rises and sharks are around.
His voice has a timid and tremulous sound.

I passed by his garden, and marked, with one eye.
How the Owl and the Panther were sharing a pie:
The Panther took pie-crust, and gravy, and meat,
While the Owl had the dish as its share of the treat.
When the pie was all finished, the Owl, as a boon,
Was kindly permitted to pocket the spoon:
While the Panther received knife and fork with a growl,
And concluded the banquet by—

THE LOBSTER QUADRILLE

'WILL you walk a little faster?' said a whiting to a snail,
'There's a porpoise close behind us, and he's treading on my tail.
See how eagerly the lobsters and the turtles all advance!
They are waiting on the shingle—
    will you come and join the dance?
Will you, won't you, will you, won't you,
    will you join the dance?
Will you, won't you, will you, won't you,
    won't you join the dance?

'You can really have no notion how delightful it will be,
When they take us up and throw us, with the lobsters, out to sea!'
But the snail replied 'Too far, too far!' and gave a look askance—
Said he thanked the whiting kindly, but
    he would not join the dance.
Would not, could not, would not, could not,
    would not join the dance.
Would not, could not, would not, could not,
    could not join the dance.

'What matters it how far we go?' his scaly friend replied.
'There is another shore, you know, upon the other side.
The further off from England the nearer is to France—
Then turn not pale, beloved snail,
    but come and join the dance.
Will you, won't you, will you, won't you,
    will you join the dance?
Will you, won't you, will you, won't you,
    won't you join the dance?'

TURTLE SOUP

BEAUTIFUL Soup, so rich and green,
Waiting in a hot tureen!
Who for such dainties would not stoop?
Soup of the evening, beautiful Soup!
Soup of the evening, beautiful Soup!
    Beau–ootiful Soo–oop!
    Beau–ootiful Soo–oop!
Soo–oop of the e–e–evening,
    Beautiful, beautiful Soup!

Beautiful Soup! Who cares for fish,
Game, or any other dish?
Who would not give all else for two p
ennyworth only of beautiful Soup?
Pennyworth only of beautiful Soup?
    Beau–ootiful Soo–oop !
    Beau–ootiful Soo–oop !
Soo-oop of the e–e–evening,
    Beautiful, beauti–FUL SOUP!

A SORT OF LULLABY

SPEAK roughly to your little boy,
  And beat him when he sneezes:
He only does it to annoy,
  Because he knows it teases.
        CHORUS
      Wow! wow! wow!

I speak severely to my boy,
  I beat him when he sneezes;
For he can thoroughly enjoy
  The pepper when he pleases!
        CHORUS
      Wow! wow! wow!

EXCELSIOR

The elder and the younger knight,
  They sallied forth at three;
How far they went on level ground
  It matters not to me;
What time they reached the foot of hill,
  When they began to mount,
Are problems which I hold to be
  Of very small account.

The moment that each waved his hat
  Upon the topmost peak—
To trivial, query such as this
  No answer will I seek.
Yet can I tell the distance well
  They must have travelled o'er:
On hill and plain, 'twixt three and nine,
  The miles were twenty-four.

Four miles an hour their steady pace
  Along the level track,
Three when they climbed—but six when they
  Came swiftly striding back
Adown the hill; and little skill
  It needs, methinks, to show,
Up hill and down together told,
Four miles an hour they go.

For whether long or short the time
  Upon the hill they spent,
Two thirds were passed in going up,
  One third in the descent.
Two thirds at three, one third at six,
  If rightly reckoned o'er,
Will make one whole at four—the tale
  Is tangled now no more.

ALGEBRAIC POEM

YET what are all such gaieties to me
Whose thoughts are full of indices and surds?
$x^2 + 7x + 53$

$= 11/3$

THE NEW BELFRY OF CHRIST CHURCH, OXFORD

FIVE fathom square the Belfry frowns;
All its sides of timber made;
Painted all in grays and browns;
Nothing of it that will fade.
Christ Church may admire the change—
Oxford thinks it sad and strange.
Beauty's dead! Let's ring her knell,
Hark! now I hear them—ding-dong, bell.

MELANCHOLETTA

WITH saddest music all day long
   She soothed her secret sorrow:
At night she sighed 'I fear 'twas wrong
   Such cheerful words to borrow.
Dearest, a sweeter, sadder song
   I'll sing to thee to-morrow.'

I thanked her, but I could not say
   That I was glad to hear it:
I left the house at break of day,
   And did not venture near it
Till time, I hoped, had worn away
   Her grief, for nought could cheer it!

My dismal sister! Couldst thou know
   The wretched home thou keepest!
Thy brother, drowned in daily woe,
   Is thankful when thou sleepest;
For if I laugh, however low,
   When thou'rt awake, thou weepest!

I took my sister t'other day
   (Excuse the slang expression)
To Sadler's Wells to see the play,
   In hopes the new impression
Might in her thoughts from grave to gay
   Effect some slight digression.

I asked three gay young dogs from town
    To join us in our folly,
Whose mirth, I thought, might serve to drown
    My sister's melancholy:
The lively Jones, the sportive Brown,
    And Robinson the jolly.

The maid announced the meal in tones
    That I myself had taught her,
Meant to allay my sister's moans,
    Like oil on troubled water;
I rushed to Jones, the lively Jones,
    And begged him to escort her.

Vainly he strove, with ready wit,
    To joke about the weather—
To ventilate the last '*on dit*'—
    To quote the price of leather—
She groaned, 'Here I and Sorrow sit:
    Let us lament together!'

I urged, 'You're wasting time, you know:
    Delay will spoil the venison.'
'My heart is wasted with my woe!
    There is no rest—in Venice, on
The Bridge of Sighs!' she quoted low,
    From Byron and from Tennyson.

I need not tell of soup and fish,
    In solemn silence swallowed,
The sobs that ushered in each dish,
    And its departure followed;
Nor yet my suicidal wish
    To *be* the cheese I hollowed.

Some desperate attempts were made
　　To start a conversation;
'Madam,' the sportive Brown essayed,
　　'Which kind of recreation,
Hunting or fishing, have you made
　　Your special occupation?'

Her lips curved downwards instantly,
　　As if of india-rubber.
'Hounds *in full cry* I like', said she:
　　(Oh, how I longed to snub her!)
Of fish, a whale's the one for me,
　　It is so full of blubber!'

The night's performance was 'King John'.
　　'It's dull', she wept, 'and so-so!'
Awhile I let her tears flow on,
　　She said they soothed her woe so!
At length the curtain rose upon
　　'Bombastes Furioso'.

In vain we roared; in vain we tried
　　To rouse her into laughter:
Her pensive glances wandered wide,
　　From orchestra to rafter—
'Tier upon Tier!' she said, and sighed;
　　And silence followed after.

YOU ARE OLD, FATHER WILLIAM

'You are old, Father William,' the young man said,
   'And your hair has become very white;
And yet you incessantly stand on your head—
   Do you think, at your age, it is right?'

'In my youth', Father William replied to his son,
   'I feared it might injure the brain;
But, now that I'm perfectly sure I have none,
   Why, I do it again and again.'

'You are old,' said the youth, 'as I mentioned before,
   And have grown most uncommonly fat;
Yet you turned a back-somersault in at the door—
   Pray, what is the reason of that?'

'In my youth', said the sage, as he shook his grey locks,
   'I kept all my limbs very supple
By the use of this ointment—one shilling the box—
   Allow me to sell you a couple?'

'You are old,' said the youth, 'and your jaws are too weak
   For anything tougher than suet;
Yet you finished the goose, with the bones and the beak—
   Pray how did you manage to do it?'

'In my youth', said his father, 'I took to the law,
   And argued each case with my wife;
And the muscular strength, which it gave to my jaw,
   Has lasted the rest of my life.'

'You are old,' said the youth, 'one would hardly suppose
   That your eye was as steady as ever;
Yet you balanced an eel on the end of your nose—
   What made you so awfully clever?'

'I have answered three questions, and that is enough,'
   Said his father; 'don't give yourself airs!
Do you think I can listen all day to such stuff?
   Be off, or I'll kick you down stairs!'

POETA FIT, NON NASCITUR

How shall I be a poet?
    How shall I write in rhyme?
You told me once 'the very wish
    Partook of the sublime'.
Then tell me how! Don't put me off
    With your 'another time'!

The old man smiled to see him,
    To hear his sudden sally;
He liked the lad to speak his mind
    Enthusiastically;
And thought, 'There's no hum-drum in him,
    Nor any shilly-shally'.

'And would you be a poet
    Before you've been to school?
Ah, well! I hardly thought you
    So absolute a fool.
First learn to be spasmodic—
    A very simple rule.

'For first you write a sentence,
    And then you chop it small;
Then mix the bits, and sort them out
    Just as they chance to fall:
The order of the phrases makes
    No difference at all.

'Then, if you'd be impressive,
  Remember what I say,
That abstract qualities begin
  With capitals alway:
The True, the Good, the Beautiful—
  Those are the things that pay!

'Next, when you are describing
  A shape, or sound, or tint;
Don't state the matter plainly,
  But put it in a hint;
And learn to look at all things
  With a sort of mental squint.'

'For instance, if I wished, Sir,
  Of mutton-pies to tell,
Should I say, "dreams of fleecy flocks
  Pent in a wheaten cell"?
'Why, yes,' the old man said: 'that phrase
  Would answer very well.

'Then fourthly, there are epithets
  That suit with any word—
As well as Harvey's Reading Sauce
  With fish, or flesh, or bird—
Of these, "wild", "lonely", "weary", "strange",
  Are much to be preferred.'

'And will it do, oh, will it do
  To take them in a lump—
As "the wild man went his weary way
  To a strange and lonely pump"?'
'Nay, nay! You must not hastily
  To such conclusions jump.

'Such epithets, like pepper,
  Give zest to what you write;
And, if you strew them sparely,
  They whet the appetite;
But if you lay them on too thick,
  You spoil the matter quite!

'Last, as to the arrangement:
  Your reader, you should show him,
Must take what information he
  Can get, and look for no im-
mature disclose of the drift
  And purpose of your poem.

'Therefore, to test his patience—
  How much he can endure—
Mention no places, names, or dates,
  And evermore be sure
Throughout the poem to be found
  Consistently obscure.

'First fix upon the limit
  To which it shall extend:
Then fill it up with "Padding"
  (Beg some of any friend):
Your great SENSATION-STANZA
  You place towards the end.'

'And what is a Sensation,
  Grandfather, tell me, pray?
I think I never heard the word
  So used before to-day:
Be kind enough to mention one
  "*Exempli gratiâ*".'

And the old man, looking sadly
    Across the garden-lawn,
Where here and there a dew-drop
    Yet glittered in the dawn,
Said, 'Go to the Adelphi,
    And see the "Colleen Bawn".

'The word is due to Boucicault—
    The theory is his,
Where Life becomes a Spasm,
    And History a Whiz:
If that is not Sensation,
    I don't know what it is.

'Now try your hand, ere Fancy
    Have lost its present glow—'
'And then', his grandson added,
    'We'll publish it, you know:
Green cloth—gold-lettered at the back—
    In duodecimo!'

Then proudly smiled that old man
    To see the eager lad
Rush madly for his pen and ink
    And for his blotting-pad—
But, when he thought of *publishing*,
    His face grew stern and sad.